This journal belongs to

....

© 2009 Ellie Claire Gift & Paper Corp.
www.ellieclaire.com

Compiled by Marilyn Jansen
Designed by Lisa & Jeff Franke

ISBN 978-1-935416-08-1

Printed in China

Proverbs

JOURNAL

Ellie Claire

gift & paper expressions

...inspired by life

The Tablet of Your Heart

Those who are steadily learning how to love are
enabled to do this because the very love of God,
Himself, has been put into our hearts.

EUGENIA PRICE

Let love and faithfulness never leave you;
bind them around your neck,
write them on the tablet of your heart.
Then you will win favor and a good name
in the sight of God and man.
Trust in the LORD with all your heart
and lean not on your own understanding;
in all your ways acknowledge him,
and he will make your paths straight.

PROVERBS 3:3-6 NIV

The Tablet of Your Heart

The Common Sense of Faith

True friendship with God...means being so intimately
in touch with God that you never even need to ask Him
to show you His will. You are God's will. And all of your
seemingly commonsense decisions are actually His
will for you, unless you sense a check in your spirit.

OSWALD CHAMBERS

Dear friend,
guard Clear Thinking and Common Sense with your life;
don't for a minute lose sight of them.
They'll keep your soul alive and well,
they'll keep you fit and attractive.

PROVERBS 3:21-22 THE MESSAGE

Faith declares what the senses do not see,
but not the contrary of what they see.
It is above them, not contrary to them.

BLAISE PASCAL

The Common Sense of Faith

A Bright Start

We can get a right start only by accepting God as
He is and learning to love Him for what He is.
As we go on to know Him better we shall find it a source
of unspeakable joy that God is just what He is.

A. W. TOZER

Even a child is known by his doings,
whether his work be pure, and whether it be right.

PROVERBS 20:11 KJV

Wise is he who can take the little moment as it
comes and make it brighter ere 'tis gone.

DANIEL ORCUTT

The ways of right-living people glow with light;
the longer they live, the brighter they shine.

PROVERBS 4:18 THE MESSAGE

A Bright Start

Speak Carefully

For attractive lips,
Speak words of kindness.

SAM LEVENSON

Kind words are like honey—
sweet to the soul and healthy for the body.

PROVERBS 16:24 NLT

Sometimes it is necessary for us to speak.
At other times it is important that we be quiet.
Wisdom comes with knowing the difference.

MRS. D. E. CLAY

Gold there is, and rubies in abundance,
but lips that speak knowledge are a rare jewel.

PROVERBS 20:15 NIV

Talking comes by nature, silence by wisdom.

AMERICAN PROVERB

Whoever keeps his mouth and his tongue
keeps himself out of trouble.

PROVERBS 21:23 ESV

Speak Carefully

The Making of a Life

The wise don't expect to find life worth living;
they make it that way.

The LORD brought me forth as the first of his works,
before his deeds of old;
I was appointed from eternity,
from the beginning, before the world began.
When there were no oceans, I was given birth,
when there were no springs abounding with water;
before the mountains were settled in place,
before the hills, I was given birth,
before he made the earth or its fields
or any of the dust of the world.

PROVERBS 8:22-26 NIV

From what we get, we can make a living;
what we give, however, makes a life.

ARTHUR ASHE

The Making of a Life

Friends Stick Together

Friends are an indispensable part of a meaningful life.
They are the ones who share our burdens and multiply our blessings.
A true friend sticks by us in our joys and sorrows. In good times
and bad, we need friends who will pray for us, listen to us,
and lend a comforting hand and an understanding ear when needed.

BEVERLY LAHAYE

There are "friends" who destroy each other,
but a real friend sticks closer than a brother.

PROVERBS 18:24 NLT

A friend is somebody who loves us with understanding,
as well as emotion.

ROBERT LOUIS STEVENSON

Friends Stick Together

Trust God's Process

Listen to my instruction and be wise;
do not ignore it.

PROVERBS 8:33 NIV

God is here. I have joyously discovered that He is always
"up to something" in my life, and I am learning to
quit second-guessing Him and simply trust the process.

GLORIA GAITHER

The teaching of the wise is a fountain of life,
that one may turn away from the snares of death.

PROVERBS 13:14 ESV

You can never change the past. But by the grace of God,
you can win the future. So remember those things
which will help you forward, but forget
those things which will only hold you back.

RICHARD C. WOODSOME

Trust God's Process

_____

_____

_____

_____

_____

_____

_____

_____

_____

_____

_____

_____

_____

_____

_____

_____

He Is the Source

I abide in Christ and in doing so I find rest, and the peace of
God which passes all understanding fills my heart and life.

JOHN HUNTER

*C*harm is deceptive, and beauty is fleeting;
but a woman who fears the LORD is to be praised.
Give her the reward she has earned,
and let her works bring her praise at the city gate.

PROVERBS 31:30-31 NIV

*H*e is the Source. Of everything. Strength for your day.
Wisdom for your task. Comfort for your soul.
Grace for your battle. Provision for each need.
Understanding for each failure. Assistance for every encounter.

JACK HAYFORD

He Is the Source

....

....

....

....

....

....

....

....

....

....

....

....

....

....

....

....

....

....

....

....

Safe in God

We do not understand the intricate pattern of the stars
in their courses, but we know that He who created
them does, and that just as surely as He guides them,
He is charting a safe course for us.

BILLY GRAHAM

Have no fear of sudden disaster
or of the ruin that overtakes the wicked,
for the Lord will be your confidence
and will keep your foot from being snared.

PROVERBS 3:25-26 NIV

When we are told that God, who is our dwelling place,
is also our fortress, it can only mean one thing, and that is that if we
will but live in our dwelling place, we shall be perfectly safe and
secure from every assault of every possible enemy that can attack us.

HANNAH WHITALL SMITH

Safe in God

....
....
....
....
....
....
....
....
....
....
....
....
....
....
....

The Wisdom of Advice

Pride only breeds quarrels,
but wisdom is found in those who take advice.

PROVERBS 13:10 NIV

A true friend...advises justly, assists readily,
adventures boldly, takes all patiently, defends
courageously, and continues a friend unchangeably.

WILLIAM PENN

Without wise leadership, a nation falls;
there is safety in having many advisers.

PROVERBS 11:14 NLT

Many receive advice; only the wise profit from it.

PUBLILIUS SYRUS

The right word at the right time
is like a custom-made piece of jewelry,
and a wise friend's timely reprimand
is like a gold ring slipped on your finger.

PROVERBS 25:11-12 THE MESSAGE

The Wisdom of Advice

....

....

....

....

....

....

....

....

....

....

....

....

....

A Wise Life

*H*e who walks with the wise grows wise.

ARISTOPHANES

PROVERBS 13:20 NIV

*W*ise people, even though all laws were abolished,
would still lead the same life.

ARISTOPHANES

I, wisdom, dwell together with prudence;
I possess knowledge and discretion.
To fear the LORD is to hate evil;
I hate pride and arrogance,
evil behavior and perverse speech.
Counsel and sound judgment are mine;
I have understanding and power.

PROVERBS 8:12-14 NIV

*I*f only man could get a little older a little later,
and a little wiser a little younger.

DICK GREGORY

A Wise Life

Remember Joy

There is joy in heaven when a tear of sorrow is shed
in the presence of a truly understanding heart.
And heaven will never forget that joy.

CHARLES MALIK

The prospect of the righteous is joy,
but the hopes of the wicked come to nothing.

PROVERBS 10:28 NIV

A part of our petition must always be for an increasing
discernment so that we can see things as God sees them.
We may ask for greater faith so that we can heal others,
but God, who understands human need far better than we do,
gives us greater compassion so that we can weep with others.

RICHARD J. FOSTER

Remember Joy

Common Wisdom

I guide you in the way of wisdom
and lead you along straight paths.
When you walk, your steps will not be hampered;
when you run, you will not stumble.

PROVERBS 4:11-12 NIV

God give me joy in the common things:
In the dawn that lures, the eve that sings.....
In the songs of children, unrestrained;
In the sober wisdom age has gained.
God give me joy in the tasks that press,
In the memories that burn and bless;
In the thought that life has love to spend,
In the faith that God's at journey's end.
God give me hope for each day that springs,
God give me joy in the common things!

THOMAS CURTIS CLARK

Common Wisdom

Eternal Dignity

She is clothed with strength and dignity;
she can laugh at the days to come.
She speaks with wisdom,
and faithful instruction is on her tongue.

PROVERBS 31:25-26 NIV

The truth [is] that there is only one
terminal dignity—love.
And the story of a love is not important—
what is important is that one is
capable of love. It is perhaps the only
glimpse we are permitted of eternity.

HELEN HAYES

Love prospers when a fault is forgiven,
but dwelling on it separates close friends.

PROVERBS 17:9 NLT

Eternal Dignity

The Blessing of Friends

A friend loveth at all times.

PROVERBS 17:17 KJV

I account that one of the greatest demonstrations of real friendship,
that a friend can really endeavor to have his friend advanced in honor,
in reputation, in the opinion of wit or learning, before himself.

JEREMY TAYLOR

*P*erfume and incense bring joy to the heart,
and the pleasantness of one's friend
springs from his earnest counsel.

PROVERBS 27:9 NIV

*W*hat a blessing is a friend with a heart so trustworthy that you
may safely bury all your secrets in it, whose conscience you may
fear less than your own, who can relieve your cares by his words,
your doubts by his advice, your sadness by his good humor,
and whose very look gives comfort to you.

The Blessing of Friends

Loving Instruction

It behooves a father to be blameless if he expects his son
to be more blameless than he was himself.

TITUS MACCIUS PLAUTUS

The righteous man leads a blameless life;
blessed are his children after him.

PROVERBS 20:7 NIV

If you have a habit of being attentive and expressing interest,
your children will not confuse your loving instruction with rejection.

CHARLES STANLEY

A fool despises his father's instruction,
But he who receives correction is prudent.
In the house of the righteous there is much treasure,
But in the revenue of the wicked is trouble.

PROVERBS 15:5-6 NKJV

Loving Instruction

_____

_____

_____

_____

_____

_____

_____

_____

_____

_____

_____

_____

_____

Timely Advice

Advice is like snow; the softer it falls the longer it dwells upon,
and the deeper it sinks into the mind.

SAMUEL TAYLOR COLERIDGE

Get advice if you want your plans to work.
If you go to war, get the advice of others.

PROVERBS 20:18 NCV

Take the advice of a faithful friend, and submit
thy inventions to his censure.

THOMAS FULLER

A man finds joy in giving an apt reply—
and how good is a timely word!

PROVERBS 15:23 NIV

All that is required to build a stable relationship is the desire
to do so...with a little advice and counsel. Ultimately, of course,
we will rely on the principles endorsed by the creator of
families Himself. That is pretty safe counsel.

JAMES DOBSON

Timely Advice

Humble in His Sight

As we enter more and more deeply into this experience of
being humbled and exalted, our knowledge of God increases,
and with it our peace, our strength, and our joy. God help us,
then, to put our knowledge about God to this use,
that we all may in truth "know the Lord."

J. I. PACKER

The fear of the LORD teaches a man wisdom,
and humility comes before honor.

PROVERBS 15:33 NIV

Teach me, O LORD, to do Your will;
teach me to live worthily and humbly
in Your sight; for You are my Wisdom.

THOMAS À KEMPIS

Commit your work to the LORD,
and your plans will be established.

PROVERBS 16:3 ESV

Humble in His Sight

Well Done

Well-spoken words bring satisfaction;
well-done work has its own reward.

PROVERBS 12:14 THE MESSAGE

There is much satisfaction in work well done;
praise is sweet, but there can be no happiness equal to
the joy of finding a heart that understands.

VICTOR ROBINSON

Good friend, don't forget all I've taught you;
take to heart my commands.
They'll help you live a long, long time,
a long life lived full and well.

PROVERBS 3:1-2 THE MESSAGE

I would give more for the private esteem and love of one
than for the public praise of ten thousand.

W. E. ALGER

Well Done

Righteousness Is an Inside Job

He who sows righteousness reaps a sure reward....
Those who are righteous will go free.

PROVERBS 11:18, 21 NIV

Righteousness alone brings lasting peace.

THELMA GRAY

The mouth of the righteous is a fountain of life,
but the mouth of the wicked conceals violence.
Hatred stirs up strife,
but love covers all offenses.

PROVERBS 10:11-12 ESV

The needed change within us is God's work, not ours.
The demand is for an inside job, and only God can work
from the inside. We cannot attain or earn this righteousness
of the kingdom of God: it is a grace that is given.

RICHARD J. FOSTER

Righteousness Is an Inside Job

The Gift of Friends

A word of encouragement to those we meet, a cheerful smile
in the supermarket, a card or letter to a friend, a readiness
to witness when opportunity is given—all are practical ways
in which we may let His light shine through us.

ELIZABETH B. JONES

A cheerful look brings joy to the heart;
good news makes for good health.

PROVERBS 15:30 NLT

Friendship is meeting another's needs in a practical way.

BEVERLY LaHAYE

Everyone is the friend of a man who gives gifts.

PROVERBS 19:6 NIV

The Gift of Friends

True Understanding

For the LORD gives wisdom,
and from his mouth come knowledge and understanding.
He holds victory in store for the upright,
he is a shield to those whose walk is blameless,
for he guards the course of the just
and protects the way of his faithful ones.

PROVERBS 2:6-8 NIV

It is never enough to know about spiritual things
with your mind. Mental knowledge is not the same
thing as truly understanding from the center of
your being, which results from experiencing and doing.

TERESA OF AVILA

Joyful is the person who finds wisdom,
the one who gains understanding.
For wisdom is more profitable than silver,
and her wages are better than gold.

PROVERBS 3:13-14 NLT

True Understanding

Keep to God's Path

*L*isten, my son, and be wise,
and keep your heart on the right path.

PROVERBS 23:19 NIV

*M*ake no little plans; they have no magic to stir men's blood
and probably themselves will not be realized. Make big plans;
aim high in hope and work, remembering that a noble,
logical diagram once recorded will not die.

DANIEL H. BURNHAM

*I*n his heart a man plans his course,
but the LORD determines his steps.

PROVERBS 16:9 NIV

*G*od's wisdom is always available to help us choose from alternatives
we face, and help us to follow His eternal plan for us.

GLORIA GAITHER

*T*he very steps we take come from GOD;
otherwise how would we know where we're going?

PROVERBS 20:24 THE MESSAGE

Keep to God's Path

Sharpen Your Character

Courage is what it takes to stand up and speak;
courage is also what it takes to sit down and listen.

WINSTON CHURCHILL

Speak up for those who cannot speak for themselves,
for the rights of all who are destitute.

PROVERBS 31:8 NIV

The firmest friendships have been formed in mutual adversity;
as iron is most strongly united by the fiercest flame.

COLTON

As iron sharpens iron,
so a friend sharpens a friend.

PROVERBS 27:17 NLT

A good friend will sharpen your character, draw your soul into
the light, and challenge your heart to love in a greater way.

Sharpen Your Character

_____

_____

_____

_____

_____

_____

_____

_____

_____

_____

_____

_____

_____

Worry No More

An anxious heart weighs a man down,
but a kind word cheers him up.

PROVERBS 12:25 NIV

You can learn to overcome the worry of anticipation.
After you begin to experience more and more the ready success
of divine grace upon all occasions, you will not worry about things
before they happen. When the time comes for you to do your duty,
you will find God as in a clear mirror, and He will empower you
and make you fit to fulfill your obligations.

BROTHER LAWRENCE

Just as water mirrors your face,
so your face mirrors your heart.

PROVERBS 27:19 THE MESSAGE

Worry No More

Eternal Safety

For the simple are killed by their turning away,
and the complacency of fools destroys them;
but whoever listens to me will dwell secure
and will be at ease, without dread of disaster.

PROVERBS 1:32-33 ESV

We shall steer safely through every storm, so long as our
heart is right, our intention fervent, our courage steadfast,
and our trust fixed on God.

FRANCIS DE SALES

The fear of the LORD is a fountain of life,
turning a man from the snares of death.

PROVERBS 14:27 NIV

With God, life is eternal—both in quality and length.
There is no joy comparable to the joy of discovering
something new from God, about God. If the continuing life
is a life of joy, we will go on discovering, learning.

EUGENIA PRICE

Eternal Safety

He Is My Wisdom

Teach me, O Lord, to do Your will; teach me to live worthily
and humbly in Your sight; for You are my Wisdom,
who knew me truly, and who knew me before
the world was made, and before I had my being.

THOMAS À KEMPIS

If you accept my words
and store up my commands within you,
turning your ear to wisdom
and applying your heart to understanding,
and if you call out for insight
and cry aloud for understanding,
and if you look for it as for silver
and search for it as for hidden treasure,
then you will understand the fear of the LORD
and find the knowledge of God.

PROVERBS 2:1-5 NIV

He Is My Wisdom

Good Understanding

Obey my commands and live!
Guard my instructions as you guard your own eyes.
Tie them on your fingers as a reminder.
Write them deep within your heart.
Love wisdom like a sister;
make insight a beloved member of your family.

PROVERBS 7:2-4 NLT

Communication is the meeting of meaning. When your
meaning meets my meaning across the bridge of words,
tones, acts, and deeds, when understanding occurs,
then we know that we have communicated.

DAVID AUGSBURGER

Good understanding wins favor.

PROVERBS 13:15 NIV

A conflict cannot be entered with the idea that one must "win."
There is no winning or losing in a good conflict,
but a breaking through to better understanding of each other.

CAROLE MAYHALL

Good Understanding

What to Do Next

How much better to get wisdom than gold,
and good judgment than silver!
The path of the virtuous leads away from evil;
whoever follows that path is safe.

PROVERBS 16:16-17 NLT

Compassionate the mountains rise
Dim with the wistful dimness of old eyes
That, having looked on life time out of mind,
Know that the simple gift of being kind
Is greater than all wisdom of the wise.

DUBOSE HEYWARD

He who gets wisdom loves his own soul;
he who cherishes understanding prospers.

PROVERBS 19:8 NIV

Wisdom oft times consists of knowing what to do next.

HERBERT HOOVER

What to Do Next

Stay True

If we can but for a moment see our mate
as God does, our compassion and love and
understanding may be changed for a lifetime.
A new view of our mate can only be
accomplished as God gives it to us by His grace,
and that grace is tapped through prayer.

JAMES DOBSON

Do you know the saying, "Drink from your own rain barrel,
draw water from your own spring-fed well"?
It's true. Otherwise, you may one day come home
and find your barrel empty and your well polluted.

PROVERBS 5:15-16 THE MESSAGE

So live that when your spouse says he/she is married to you,
he/she will be boasting.

Stay True

Silent Times

The wise in heart are called discerning,
and pleasant words promote instruction.

PROVERBS 16:21 NIV

True friendship thrives through media
Of touch and sight and speech,
But often in the silent times
It most extends its reach.

CRAIG E. SATHOFF

Even fools are thought wise when they keep silent;
with their mouths shut, they seem intelligent.

PROVERBS 17:28 NLT

Silent Times

Cling to Wisdom

*L*ife is so generous a giver,
but we, judging its gifts
by the covering,
cast them away as ugly,
or heavy or hard.
Remove the covering
and you will find beneath it
a living splendor,
woven of love,
by wisdom, with power.

Frà Giovanni

*D*on't turn your back on wisdom,
for she will protect you.
Love her, and she will guard you.
Getting wisdom is the wisest thing you can do!
And whatever else you do, develop good judgment.

Proverbs 4:6-7 nlt

Cling to Wisdom

Power to Do Good

If you can help anybody even a little, be glad;
up the steps of usefulness and kindness,
God will lead you on to happiness and friendship.

MALTBIE D. BABCOCK

Do not withhold good from those who deserve it
when it's in your power to help them.

PROVERBS 3:27 NLT

Encouragement is being a good listener, being positive,
letting others know you accept them for who they are. It is offering
hope, caring about the feelings of another, understanding.

GIGI GRAHAM TCHIVIDJIAN

A good person gives life to others;
the wise person teaches others how to live.

PROVERBS 11:30 NCV

Power to Do Good

....

....

....

....

....

....

....

....

....

....

....

....

....

....

....

....

....

....

....

....

Loving Correction

The Lord corrects those he loves,
just as parents correct the child they delight in.

PROVERBS 3:12 NCV

Heavenly Father,
Teach me how to properly and fairly discipline my children,
so that I may bring them to an understanding of Your authority
in their lives. As they grow older, may the guidelines and
principles I have taught them lead them to a life of self-control
based on following Your commandments. Amen.

KIM BOYCE

Discipline your children,
and they will give you peace of mind
and will make your heart glad.

PROVERBS 29:17 NLT

Loving Correction

....

....

....

....

....

....

....

....

....

....

....

....

....

....

Safe and Secure

When you lie down, you won't be afraid;
when you lie down, you will sleep in peace.

PROVERBS 3:24 NCV

May the God of love and peace set your heart at rest and
speed you on your journey. May He meanwhile shelter you
from disturbance by others in the place of complete plenitude
where you will repose for ever in the vision of peace,
in the security of trust and in the restful enjoyment of His riches.

RAYMOND OF PENYAFORT

Those who respect the Lord will have security,
and their children will be protected.

PROVERBS 14:26 NCV

Safe and Secure

Look With Love

God looks at the world through the eyes of love. If we, therefore, as human beings made in the image of God also want to see reality rationally, that is, as it truly is, then we, too, must learn to look at what we see with love.

ROBERTA BONDI

I love those who love me,
And those who seek me diligently will find me.
Riches and honor are with me,
Enduring riches and righteousness.
My fruit is better than gold, yes, than fine gold,
And my revenue than choice silver.
I traverse the way of righteousness,
In the midst of the paths of justice,
That I may cause those who love me to inherit wealth,
That I may fill their treasuries.

PROVERBS 8:17-21 NKJV

Look With Love

Written on My Heart

If God exists and we are made in His image we can have
real meaning, and we can have real knowledge through what
He has communicated to us.

FRANCIS SCHAEFFER

Hold on to instruction, do not let it go;
guard it well, for it is your life.

PROVERBS 4:13 NIV

What keeps the Christian going...is the knowledge
of God written on his or her heart.

LINDA CLARK

Apply your heart to instruction
and your ears to words of knowledge.

PROVERBS 23:12 NIV

God is constantly taking knowledge of me in love,
and watching over me for my good.

J. I. PACKER

Written on My Heart

What Can I Give?

What can I give Him
Poor as I am?
If I were a shepherd,
I would give Him a lamb,
If I were a Wise Man,
I would do my part,—
But what I can I give Him,
Give my heart.

CHRISTINA ROSSETTI

He who is kind to the poor lends to the LORD,
and he will reward him for what he has done.

PROVERBS 19:17 NIV

God often calls us to do things that we do not have the
ability to do. Spiritual discernment is knowing if God calls
you to do something, God empowers you to do it.

SUZANNE FARNHAM

The wise in heart are called discerning,
and pleasant words promote instruction.

PROVERBS 16:21 NIV

What Can I Give?

Honest Words

*G*ood leaders cultivate honest speech;
they love advisors who tell them the truth.

PROVERBS 16:13 THE MESSAGE

*A*s light is pleasant to the eye, so is truth
to the understanding.

RICHARD PELHAM

*A*n honest answer is like
a kiss on the lips.

PROVERBS 24:26 NIV

*G*od be in my mouth,
And in my speaking;
God be in my heart,
And in my thinking.

BILLY GRAHAM

A wise man's heart guides his mouth.

PROVERBS 16:23 NIV

Honest Words

Work Diligently

Learning is not attained by chance, it must be
sought for with ardor and attended to with diligence.

ABIGAIL ADAMS

Lazy people don't even cook the game they catch,
but the diligent make use of everything they find.

PROVERBS 12:27 NLT

Thank God every morning when you get up that you have
something to do that day which must be done, whether you
like it or not. Being forced to work, and forced to do your best,
will breed in you temperance and self-control,
diligence and strength of will, cheerfulness and contentment,
and a hundred virtues which the idle never know.

CHARLES KINGSLEY

The plans of the diligent lead to profit
as surely as haste leads to poverty.

PROVERBS 21:5 NIV

Work Diligently

....

....

....

....

....

....

....

....

....

....

....

....

Pray with Conviction

The LORD approves of those who are good,
but he condemns those who plan wickedness.

PROVERBS 12:2 NLT

Keep praying, but be thankful that God's
answers are wiser than your prayers!

WILLIAM CULBERTSON

A faithful man will abound with blessings.

PROVERBS 28:20 ESV

How vital that we pray, armed with the knowledge that God
is in heaven. Pray with any lesser conviction and your prayers
are timid, shallow, and hollow. But spend some time walking
in the workshop of the heavens, seeing what God has done,
and watch how your prayers are energized.

MAX LUCADO

Pray with Conviction

....

....

....

....

....

....

....

....

....

....

....

....

....

....

Discerning the Holy

The discerning sets his face toward wisdom,
but the eyes of a fool are on the ends of the earth.

PROVERBS 17:24 ESV

God wants us to be present where we are.
He invites us to see and to hear what is around us and,
through it all, to discern the footprints of the Holy.

RICHARD J. FOSTER

The heart of the discerning acquires knowledge;
the ears of the wise seek it out.

PROVERBS 18:15 NIV

To acquire knowledge, one must study;
but to acquire wisdom, one must observe.

MARILYN VOS SAVANT

Discerning the Holy

Loyal Friends

Reliable friends who do what they say
are like cool drinks in sweltering heat—refreshing!
Like billowing clouds that bring no rain
is the person who talks big but never produces.

PROVERBS 25:13-14 THE MESSAGE

Talk not of wasted affection!
Affection never was wasted;
If it enrich not the heart of another,
its water, returning
Back to their springs, like the rain,
shall fill them full of refreshment:
That which the fountain sends forth
returns again to the fountain.

LONGFELLOW

An unreliable messenger stumbles into trouble,
but a reliable messenger brings healing.

PROVERBS 13:17 NLT

A true friend is distinguished in the crisis of hazard
and necessity; when the gallantry of his aid may show
the worth of his soul and the loyalty of his heart.

ENNIUS

Loyal Friends

Wisdom and Understanding

*A*ll [God's] glory and beauty come from within,
and there He delights to dwell.
His visits there are frequent,
His conversation sweet,
His comforts refreshing,
His peace passing all understanding.

THOMAS à KEMPIS

*B*uy the truth, and do not sell it,
Also wisdom and instruction and understanding.

PROVERBS 23:23 NKJV

*K*nowledge is proud that it knows so much;
wisdom is humble that it knows no more.

WILLIAM COWPER

*W*ise people store up knowledge,
But the mouth of the foolish is near destruction.

PROVERBS 10:14 NKJV

Wisdom and Understanding

Treasure Justice

When justice is done, it brings joy to the righteous.

PROVERBS 21:15 NIV

His justice is full and complete,
His mercy to us has no end;
the clouds are a path for His feet,
He comes on the wings of the wind.

CHRISTOPHER IDLE

You can find me on Righteous Road—that's where I walk—
at the intersection of Justice Avenue,
Handing out life to those who love me,
filling their arms with life—armloads of life!

PROVERBS 8:20-21 THE MESSAGE

Justice and power must be brought together,
so that whatever is just may be powerful,
and whatever is powerful may be just.

BLAISE PASCAL

Treasure Justice

The Beauty of the Lord

A cheerful disposition is good for your health.

PROVERBS 17:22 THE MESSAGE

I have learned from experience that the greater
part of our happiness or misery depends on our
dispositions and not on our circumstances.

MARTHA WASHINGTON

*W*isdom...will place a lovely wreath on your head;
she will present you with a beautiful crown.

PROVERBS 4:8-9 NLT

*W*e were made for God. Only by being in some
respect like Him, only by being a manifestation of
His beauty, lovingkindness, wisdom, or goodness,
has any earthly beloved excited our love.

C. S. LEWIS

The Beauty of the Lord

Deeper Understanding

The purposes of a man's heart are deep waters,
but a man of understanding draws them out.

PROVERBS 20:5 NIV

Reflection...enables our minds to be stretched in three different
directions—the direction that leads to a proper relationship with God,
the relationship that leads to a healthy relationship with others,
and the relationship that leads to a deeper understanding of oneself.

MARK CONNOLLY

A truly wise person uses few words;
a person with understanding is even-tempered.

PROVERBS 17:27 NLT

It might be a good idea to ask ourselves how we develop our
capacity to choose for joy. Maybe we could spend a moment
at the end of each day and decide to remember that day—
whatever may have happened—as a day to be grateful for.
In so doing we increase our heart's capacity to choose joy.

HENRI J. M. NOUWEN

Deeper Understanding

The Joy of Righteousness

As we pray...God is inviting us deeper in and higher up. There is training in righteousness, transforming power, new joy, deeper intimacy.

RICHARD J. FOSTER

Wealth is worthless in the day of wrath,
but righteousness delivers from death.
The righteousness of the blameless makes a straight way for them,
but the wicked are brought down by their own wickedness.
The righteousness of the upright delivers them,
but the unfaithful are trapped by evil desires.

PROVERBS 11:4-6 NIV

We are forgiven and righteous because of Christ's sacrifice;
therefore we are pleasing to God in spite of our failures.
Christ alone is the source of our forgiveness, freedom, joy, and purpose.

ROBERT S. McGEE

The Joy of Righteousness

Virtuous Worker

When Jesus was on earth, it wasn't an accident that He came as a blue-collar worker, nor that His parables would deal with things like sowing seed, vineyard laborers, harvesters, house building, and swine tending. In Him there is no hierarchy of importance vocationally, there's only the wise use of the talents He dispenses.

LARRY KREIDER

Do you see a man skilled in his work?
He will serve before kings;
he will not serve before obscure men.

PROVERBS 22:29 NIV

Wisdom is knowing what to do next, skill is knowing how to do it, and virtue is doing it.

DAVID STARR JORDAN

Virtuous Worker

....

....

....

....

....

....

....

....

....

....

....

....

....

....

Everyday Wisdom

The tongue of the wise uses knowledge rightly,
But the mouth of fools pours forth foolishness.

PROVERBS 15:2 NKJV

This voice that calls to us out of the everyday moments
of life is called the wisdom of God. This wisdom is
infused into nature and the laws that govern her,
and into human nature and the laws that govern it.

KEN GIRE

Wicked people are stubborn,
but good people think carefully about what they do.
There is no wisdom, understanding, or advice
that can succeed against the Lord.

PROVERBS 21:29-30 NCV

God's will is determined by His wisdom which always perceives,
and His goodness which always embraces the intrinsically good.

C. S. LEWIS

Everyday Wisdom

Listen Closely

Pay attention to my words;
listen closely to what I say.
Don't ever forget my words;
keep them always in mind.
They are the key to life for those who find them;
they bring health to the whole body.
Be careful what you think,
because your thoughts run your life.

PROVERBS 4:20-23 NCV

Look up at all the stars in the night sky and hear
your Father saying, "I carefully set each one in its place.
Know that I love you more than these."
Sit by the lake's edge, listening to the water lapping
the shore and hear your Father gently calling you
to that place near His heart.

Give instruction to a wise man, and he will be still wiser;
Teach a just man, and he will increase in learning.

PROVERBS 9:9 NKJV

Listen Closely

You Will Receive Mercy

Have confidence in God's mercy, for when you think He is
a long way from you, He is often quite near.

THOMAS À KEMPIS

If you hide your sins, you will not succeed.
If you confess and reject them, you will receive mercy.

PROVERBS 28:13 NCV

No offense by another person could possibly equal
our guilt before God, yet He has forgiven us; are we not
obligated to show the same mercy to others?

JAMES DOBSON

Doing what is right makes a nation great,
but sin will bring disgrace to any people.

PROVERBS 14:34 NCV

We may think we want justice. What we want
is mercy. We need it.

B. C. FORBES

You Will Receive Mercy

Share Love

The less we have, the more we give. Seems absurd,
but it's the logic of love.

MOTHER TERESA

A gift opens the way for the giver
and ushers him into the presence of the great.

PROVERBS 18:16 NIV

In all your growing and increasing godliness, don't forget to love.
Someone near you may need a hug more than an insight.

NEVA COYLE

The cheerful of heart has a continual feast.
Better is a little with the fear of the LORD
than great treasure and trouble with it.

PROVERBS 15:15-16 ESV

He made you so you could share in His creation,
could love and laugh and know Him.

TED GRIFFEN

Share Love

The Splendor of Generations

The mark of a good father is his compassionate understanding
of the fact that mistakes are a part of growing up.

GARY SMALLEY AND JOHN TRENT

Train a child in the way he should go,
and when he is old he will not turn from it.

PROVERBS 22:6 NIV

In youth acquire that which may requite you for the
deprivations of old age; and if you are mindful that old age
has wisdom for its food, you will so exert yourself in youth,
that your old age will not lack sustenance.

LEONARDO DA VINCI

The glory of young men is their strength,
gray hair the splendor of the old.

PROVERBS 20:29 NIV

The Splendor of Generations

Find Your Path

For a man's ways are in full view of the Lord,
and he examines all his paths.

PROVERBS 5:21 NIV

God can help me clear away the obstructions
and see clearly where the path is.

GLORIA GAITHER

The path of life leads upward for the wise;
they leave the grave behind.

PROVERBS 15:24 NLT

What we need is not new light, but new sight;
not new paths, but new strength to walk in the old ones;
not new duties but new wisdom from on High
to fulfill those that are plain before us.

Find Your Path

Love Your Enemies

Love is the only force capable of transforming
an enemy into a friend.

MARTIN LUTHER KING JR.

If your enemy is hungry, give him food to eat;
if he is thirsty, give him water to drink.
In doing this, you will heap burning coals on his head,
and the LORD will reward you.

PROVERBS 25:21-22 NIV

If we refuse to treat people as our enemies,
we have the best possible chance
of winning them to be our friends.

CATHERINE GORE

When a man's ways are pleasing to the LORD,
he makes even his enemies live at peace with him.

PROVERBS 16:7 NIV

Love Your Enemies

....

....

....

....

....

....

....

....

....

....

....

....

....

Patience and Diligence

If your determination is fixed, I do not counsel you to despair.
Few things are impossible to diligence and skill.
Great works are performed not by strength, but perseverance.

SAMUEL JOHNSON

Diligent hands will rule,
but laziness ends in slave labor.

PROVERBS 12:24 NIV

Patience and diligence, like faith, remove mountains.

WILLIAM PENN

The soul of the sluggard craves and gets nothing,
while the soul of the diligent is richly supplied.

PROVERBS 13:4 ESV

Have patience with all things, but chiefly have patience
with yourself. Do not lose courage in considering your
own imperfections but instantly set about remedying them—
every day begin the task anew.

FRANCIS DE SALES

Patience and Diligence

Guard Instruction

*H*e who obeys instructions guards his life.

PROVERBS 19:16 NIV

*Y*ou can trust the Lord too little,
but you can never trust Him too much.

*H*e who heeds the word wisely will find good,
And whoever trusts in the LORD, happy is he.

PROVERBS 16:20 NKJV

*N*either let mistakes nor wrong directions, of which every man,
in his studies and elsewhere, falls into many, discourage you.
There is precious instruction to be got by finding we were wrong.

THOMAS CARLYLE

*L*isten to advice and accept instruction,
and in the end you will be wise.

PROVERBS 19:20 NIV

Guard Instruction

Divine Ownership

There is no possession more valuable than a
good and faithful friend.

SOCRATES

Honor the LORD with your possessions,
And with the firstfruits of all your increase;
So your barns will be filled with plenty,
And your vats will overflow with new wine.

PROVERBS 3:9-10 NKJV

I am happy in having learned to distinguish between
ownership and possession. Books, pictures, and all the beauty
of the world belong to those who love and understand them—
not usually to those who possess them. All of these things
that I am entitled to I have—I own them by divine right.
So I care not a bit who possesses them.

JAMES HOWARD KEHLER

Divine Ownership

Live Generously

A loving heart is the truest wisdom.

CHARLES DICKENS

*G*enerous hands are blessed hands
because they give bread to the poor.
Kick out the troublemakers and things will quiet down;
you need a break from bickering and griping!

PROVERBS 22:9-10 THE MESSAGE

*T*he fountain of beauty is the heart, and every generous
thought illustrates the walls of your chamber.

FRANCIS QUARLES

A generous man will prosper;
he who refreshes others will himself be refreshed.

PROVERBS 11:25 NIV

*P*eople who deal with life generously and large-heartedly
go on multiplying relationships to the end.

ARTHUR CHRISTOPHER BENSON

Live Generously

Search Me, O Lord

The lamp of the LORD searches the spirit of a man;
it searches out his inmost being.

PROVERBS 20:27 NIV

I have since learned that when a baffling or painful
experience comes, the crucial thing is not always
to find the right answers, but to ask the right questions.
Self-questioning is a far more essential ingredient in
life that I ever supposed. It's the water that keeps
the modeling clay of our life from hardening into
something forever rigid and unchanging. To refuse
to ask honest questions of ourselves ultimately means
shutting ourselves off from revelation. Often it
is simply the right question at the right time
that propels us on into the journey of awakening.

SUE MONK KIDD

Search Me, O Lord

Filled with Grace

First, help me never to tell a lie.
Second, give me neither poverty nor riches!
Give me just enough to satisfy my needs.

PROVERBS 30:8 NLT

In the beginning, as we are learning to pray, our will is in a
struggle with God's will. In time, however, we begin to
enter into a grace-filled releasing of our will and a flowing
into the will of the Father.

RICHARD J. FOSTER

The righteous considers the cause of the poor,
But the wicked does not understand such knowledge.

PROVERBS 29:7 NKJV

The grace of God is equal to...the most unfavorable
circumstances. Its glory is to transform a curse into blessing
and show to men and angels of ages yet to come that
where sin abounded, grace did much more abound.

A. B. SIMPSON

Filled with Grace

Rejoice in Your Family

There is no more liberating experience than the joy of loving one's spouse and children, the confidence of being loved, and the knowledge that such love can move mountains and make nations whole.

GARY BAUER

Parents rejoice when their children turn out well;
wise children become proud parents.
So make your father happy!
Make your mother proud!

PROVERBS 23:24-25 THE MESSAGE

Biblical principles offer the most healthy approach to family living—even turning stress to our advantage.

JAMES DOBSON

Be wise, my son, and bring joy to my heart.

PROVERBS 27:11 NIV

Rejoice in Your Family

Wisdom Is Knowing

*I*t takes wisdom to have a good family, and it takes
understanding to make it strong.

PROVERBS 24:3 NCV

*K*nowledge is knowing a fact. Wisdom is knowing
what to do with that fact.

*K*now also that wisdom is sweet to your soul;
if you find it, there is a future hope for you,
and your hope will not be cut off.

PROVERBS 24:14 NIV

*W*ith God our trust can be abandoned, utterly free.
In Him are no limitations, no flaws, no weaknesses.
His judgment is perfect, His knowledge of us is perfect,
His love is perfect. God alone is trustworthy.

EUGENIA PRICE

Wisdom Is Knowing

The Lord's Purpose

The awe that we sense or ought to sense when standing
in the presence of a human being is a moment of intuition
for the likeness of God which is concealed in His essence.

ABRAHAM JOSHUA HESCHEL

The mocker seeks wisdom and finds none,
but knowledge comes easily to the discerning.

PROVERBS 14:6 NIV

God possesses infinite knowledge and an awareness which
is uniquely His. At all times, even in the midst of
any type of suffering, I can realize that He knows, loves,
watches, understands, and more than that, He has a purpose.

BILLY GRAHAM

Many are the plans in the mind of a man,
but it is the purpose of the LORD that will stand.

PROVERBS 19:21 ESV

The Lord's Purpose

My Strong Tower

Do not take over much thought for tomorrow. God, who
has led you safely on so far, will lead you on to the end.
Be altogether at rest in the loving holy confidence
which you ought to have in His heavenly Providence.

FRANCIS DE SALES

The name of the LORD is a strong tower:
the righteous run to it and are safe.

PROVERBS 18:10 NIV

It is a good and safe rule to sojourn in every place
as if you meant to spend your life there,
never omitting an opportunity of doing a kindness,
or speaking a true word, or making a friend.

JOHN RUSKIN

My Strong Tower

The Beginning of Knowledge

The fear of the LORD is the beginning of knowledge.

PROVERBS 1:7 NIV

What matters supremely is not the fact that I know God,
but the larger fact which underlies it—the fact that
He knows me. I am graven on the palms of His hands.
I am never out of His mind. All my knowledge of Him
depends on His sustained initiative in knowing me. I know Him
because He first knew me, and continues to know me.

J. I. PACKER

GOD guards knowledge with a passion,
but he'll have nothing to do with deception.

PROVERBS 22:12 THE MESSAGE

The Beginning of Knowledge

A Word to the Wise

Character is so largely affected by associations that we
cannot afford to be indifferent as to who and what our friends are.
They write their names in our albums, but they do more,
they help make us what we are. Be therefore careful in
selecting them; and when wisely selected, never sacrifice them.

M. HULBURD

Pay attention and listen to the sayings of the wise;
apply your heart to what I teach,
for it is pleasing when you keep them in your heart
and have all of them ready on your lips.
So that your trust may be in the LORD,
I teach you today, even you.

PROVERBS 22:17-19 NIV

A Word to the Wise

Quietly Trust

The fear of the LORD leads to life,
and whoever has it rests satisfied;
he will not be visited by harm.

PROVERBS 19:23 ESV

If the Lord be with us, we have no cause of fear. His eye
is upon us, His arm over us, His ear open to our prayer—
His grace sufficient, His promise unchangeable.

JOHN NEWTON

The blessing of the LORD makes a person rich,
and he adds no sorrow with it.

PROVERBS 10:22 NLT

What steps of wisdom lead us to a place of trust?
Let us look for what is good in our situation.
Minimize what is bad. Calmly, quietly trust in God.
Relax and let God take full control. Yes, quietly trust.

THELMA MCMILLAN

Quietly Trust

Fountain of Wisdom

The fear of the LORD is the beginning of wisdom,
and the knowledge of the Holy One is insight.

PROVERBS 9:10 ESV

By learning you will teach; by teaching you will learn.

LATIN PROVERB

A kind heart is a fountain of gladness, making everything
in its vicinity freshen into smiles.

WASHINGTON IRVING

The light of the righteous shines brightly,
but the lamp of the wicked is snuffed out.

PROVERBS 13:9 NIV

Fountain of Wisdom

Sweet Insight

Face your deficiencies and acknowledge them; but do not
let them master you. Let them teach you patience,
sweetness, insight. When we do the best we can, we never know
what miracle is wrought in our life, or in the life of another.

HELEN KELLER

ee

It pays to take life seriously;
things work out when you trust in GOD.
A wise person gets known for insight;
gracious words add to one's reputation.

PROVERBS 16:20-21 THE MESSAGE

To know wisdom and instruction,
to understand words of insight,
to receive instruction in wise dealing,
in righteousness, justice, and equity;
to give prudence to the simple,
knowledge and discretion to the youth.

PROVERBS 1:2-4 ESV

Sweet Insight

Stand Strong

Whenever we build our lives on values and principles
that contradict the time-honored wisdom of God's Word,
we are laying a foundation on the sand.

JAMES DOBSON

The wise have wealth and luxury,
but fools spend whatever they get.
Whoever pursues righteousness and unfailing love
will find life, righteousness, and honor.
The wise conquer the city of the strong
and level the fortress in which they trust.

PROVERBS 21:20-22 NLT

Regardless of whether we feel strong or weak in our faith,
we remember that our assurance is not based upon our ability
to conjure up some special feeling. Rather, it is built upon a
confident assurance in the faithfulness of God. We focus on
His trustworthiness and especially on His steadfast love.

RICHARD J. FOSTER

Stand Strong

Patient Love

Let us begin from this moment to acknowledge Him
in all our ways, and do everything, whatsoever we do,
as service to Him and for His glory, depending upon Him
alone for wisdom, and strength, and sweetness, and patience.

HANNAH WHITALL SMITH

A man's wisdom gives him patience;
it is to his glory to overlook an offense.

PROVERBS 19:11 NIV

Concrete reasons for loving another human being not
only need to be expressed to that person, but will also
help the person who is doing the verbalizing. Dwelling in
one's mind on logical reasons for love does not diminish
the feelings of love, but increases them.

EDITH SCHAEFFER

Wisdom is found on the lips of the discerning.

PROVERBS 10:13 NIV

Patient Love

Sincere Praise

Don't praise yourself. Let someone else do it.
Let the praise come from a stranger
and not from your own mouth.

PROVERBS 27:2 NCV

Who is more indefatiguable in toil, when there is
occasion for toil, than a friend? Who is readier to rejoice
in one's good fortune? Whose praise is sweeter? From whose
lips does one learn the truth with less pain? What fortress,
what bulwarks, what arms are more steadfast than loyal hearts?

JOHN CHRYSOSTOM

An open rebuke
is better than hidden love!
Wounds from a sincere friend
are better than many kisses from an enemy.

PROVERBS 27:5-6 NLT

Sincere Praise

The Lord Instructs

Let the wise hear and increase in learning,
and the one who understands obtain guidance,
to understand a proverb and a saying,
the words of the wise and their riddles.

PROVERBS 1:5-6 ESV

Rather than placing all the emphasis on earthly,
tangible treasures, our Lord instructs us to turn our attention
to those intangible treasures that defy destruction and cannot
be stolen—eternal treasures that keep the perspective clear.

CHARLES R. SWINDOLL

Good sense is a fountain of life to him who has it,
but the instruction of fools is folly.

PROVERBS 16:22 ESV

A wise gardener plants his seeds, then has the good sense
not to dig them up every few days to see if a crop is on the way.
Likewise, we must be patient as God brings the answers...
in His own good time.

QUIN SHERRER

The Lord Instructs

A Merry Heart

If you desire to be really happy, you must make God
your final and ultimate goal.

THOMAS À KEMPIS

Now, my children, listen to me,
because those who follow my ways are happy.

PROVERBS 8:32 NCV

A merry heart makes a cheerful countenance,
But by sorrow of the heart the spirit is broken.

PROVERBS 15:13 NKJV

The art of being happy lies in the power of extracting
happiness from common things.

HENRY WARD BEECHER

There is surely a future hope for you,
and your hope will not be cut off.

PROVERBS 23:18 NIV

A Merry Heart

Righteousness in the Heart

If there is righteousness in the heart, there will be beauty in the character. If there is beauty in the character, there will be harmony in the home. If there is harmony in the home, there will be order in the nation. When there is order in the nation, there will be peace in the world.

CHINESE PROVERB

People with integrity walk safely,
but those who follow crooked paths will slip and fall.
People who wink at wrong cause trouble,
but a bold reproof promotes peace.

PROVERBS 10:9-10 NLT

God's Word acts as a light for our paths. It can help scare off unwanted thoughts in our minds and protect us from the enemy.

GARY SMALLEY AND JOHN TRENT

Righteousness in the Heart

....

....

....

....

....

....

....

....

....

....

....

....

....

....

....

....

....

The Beauty of Marriage

Who can find a virtuous and capable wife?
She is more precious than rubies.
Her husband can trust her,
and she will greatly enrich his life.
She brings him good, not harm,
all the days of her life.

PROVERBS 31:10-12 NLT

You ought to trust me for I do not love and will never love
any woman in the world but you, and my chief desire is to link
myself to you week by week by bonds which shall ever become
more intimate and profound. Beloved, I kiss your memory—
your sweetness and beauty have cast a glory upon my life.

WINSTON CHURCHILL
(IN A LETTER TO HIS WIFE, CLEMENTINE)

The Beauty of Marriage

Honest Integrity

*Confidence in others' honesty is no light
testimony to one's own integrity.*

MICHEL DE MONTAIGNE

The way of the LORD is a stronghold to those with integrity,
but it destroys the wicked.
The godly will never be disturbed,
but the wicked will be removed from the land.
The mouth of the godly person gives wise advice,
but the tongue that deceives will be cut off.
The lips of the godly speak helpful words,
but the mouth of the wicked speaks perverse words.

PROVERBS 10:29-32 NLT

Personal perfection is impossible, but it is possible to
aim for genuineness, honesty, consistency, and moral purity,
and to frankly acknowledge it when we fail.

SUSAN ALEXANDER YATES